Community Helpers
Lifeguards

by Rebecca Pettiford

Bullfrog
Books

Ideas for Parents and Teachers

Bullfrog Books let children practice reading informational text at the earliest reading levels. Repetition, familiar words, and photo labels support early readers.

Before Reading

- Discuss the cover photo. Who might this book be about?

- Look at the picture glossary together. Read and discuss the words.

Read the Book

- "Walk" through the book and look at the photos. Let the child ask questions. Point out the photo labels.

- Read the book to the child, or have him or her read independently.

After Reading

- Prompt the child to think more. Ask: Have you ever seen a lifeguard at the beach or the pool? What was he or she doing?

Bullfrog Books are published by Jump!
5357 Penn Avenue South
Minneapolis, MN 55419
www.jumplibrary.com

Library of Congress Cataloging-in-Publication Data

Pettiford, Rebecca.
  Lifeguards / by Rebecca Pettiford.
     pages cm. — (Community helpers)
  Includes index.
  ISBN 978-1-62031-158-5 (hardcover) —
  ISBN 978-1-62496-245-5 (ebook)
  1. Lifeguards—Juvenile literature. I. Title.
  GV838.72.P48 2015
  797.200289—dc23
                                                    2014032120

Series Editor: Wendy Dieker
Series Designer: Ellen Huber
Book Designer: Anna Peterson
Photo Researcher: Anna Peterson

Photo Credits: All photos by Shutterstock except: Alamy, 12–13, 23tl; Corbis, 4; iStockPhoto, 5, 10–11, 13, 21; Thinkstock, 1, 3, 6–7, 8, 15, 23br.

Printed in the United States of America at Corporate Graphics in North Mankato, Minnesota.

Table of Contents

Lifeguards at Work

Sam wants to
be a lifeguard.

What do they do?

They watch us swim.

They keep us safe.

We play in the pool.

We play rough.

It's not safe.

Tweet!

Jen blows a whistle.

She tells us to stop.

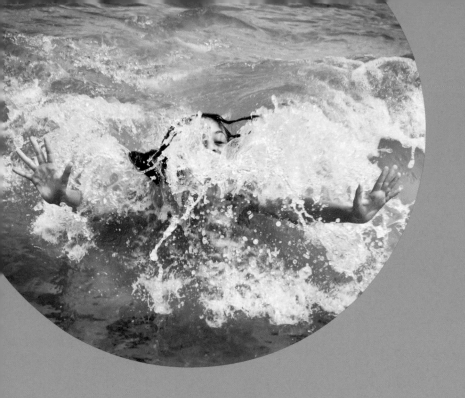

Oh no!

Ann needs help!

Kip jumps in.

He saves Ann.

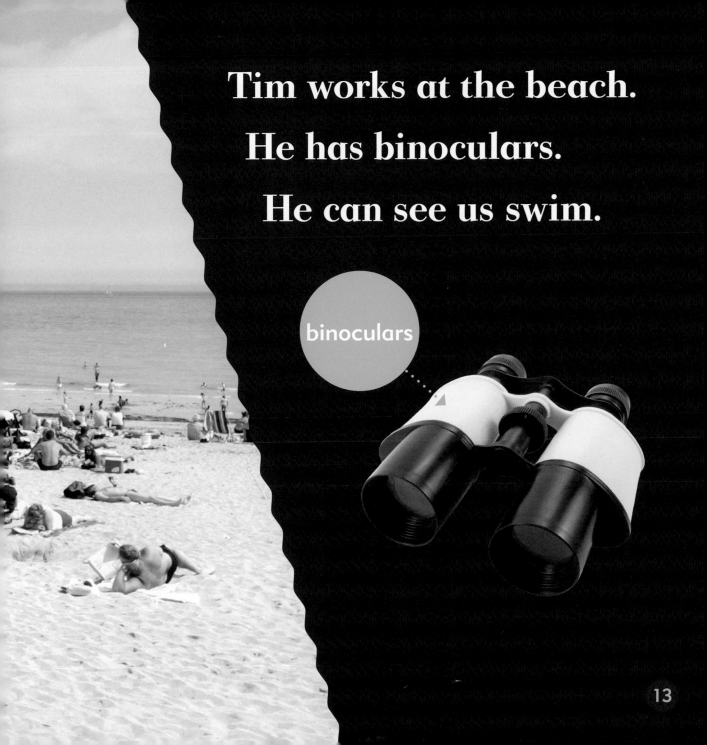

Tim works at the beach.

He has binoculars.

He can see us swim.

binoculars

Yikes!

Tim sees a shark!

14

Quick!

Get out of the water!

15

tower

rescue
board

LIFEGUARD
ON DUTY
9 AM–5 PM

SWIMMING ADVISORY
CONSEJO SOBRE NATACION

RED FLAG NO SWIMMING ADVISED
BANDERA ROJA NO SE RECOMIENDA NADA

BLUE FLAG SWIMMING ADVISED
BANDERA AZUL SE PUEDE NADAR

Ty is in a
lifeguard tower.

See his rescue board?

It floats.

He uses it to help
swimmers.

See the sign?

There is no lifeguard.

It is not safe to swim now.

The lifeguard is here. We can swim!

At the Pool

umbrella
Lifeguards sit under an umbrella for shade.

lifeguard chair
A tall chair helps lifeguards have a good view of the water.

rescue ring
Lifeguards can toss this floating ring to someone who needs help in the water.

Picture Glossary

beach
The sandy strip of land next to the water.

lifeguard tower
A high chair or shelter lifeguards use to watch swimmers.

binoculars
An instrument used to make faraway things look closer.

shark
A big ocean fish with large teeth and a large fin.

Index

To Learn More

Learning more is as easy as 1, 2, 3.

1) Go to www.factsurfer.com

2) Enter "lifeguards" into the search box.

3) Click the "Surf" button to see a list of websites.

With factsurfer.com, finding more information is just a click away.